Praying In The Spirit
The Great Adventure

by: Mark Pulley

Copyright © 2014 by Mark Pulley
All rights reserved
Printed in the United States of America
International Standard Book Number:
978-1-888081-20-6

This book or parts thereof may not be reproduced in any form without prior written permission from the author.

Published by
GOOD NEWS FELLOWSHIP MINISTRIES
220 Sleepy Creek Rd.
Macon, GA 31210
Phone: (478) 757-8071

Table of Contents

Introduction 1
Chapter 1 3
Chapter 2 58

INTRODUCTION

Acts 2:4 "And they were filled with the Holy Spirit and began to speak in other tongues as the Spirit gave them utterance."

This is the beginning of a great adventure with the Holy Spirit. Many think this is the end, or I have this gifting and that's it, but it's only the beginning of this great adventure of life in the Spirit and walking with the Holy Spirit.

Being filled with the Holy Spirit and praying in the Spirit is the beginning of adventuring out in faith to help people, and to minister with great power as Jesus did, and as the early church did. Praying in tongues, or in the Spirit, is just the beginning for this great life. It's what we need to do daily if we want this great adventure. It is not a one-time experience; it's not a religious thing to brag about; it's life in the Spirit; it's life flowing with the Holy Spirit and the Lord Jesus, so let's get ready to receive fresh revelation as we learn from the Holy Spirit, as he reveals and teaches us the Word of God and fresh insights to Jesus and the flow of the Spirit. This will not be your typical book. It is a revelation as the Holy Spirit gave it, and it is not your regular teaching type book.

Chapter 1

1 Corinthians 14:4 says, "He who prays in tongues edifies himself."

Jude: 20 says, "Building yourself up... Praying in the Spirit builds and strengthens your spirit, soul and body." Praying in the Spirit will build up and strengthen you in every area of your life. By training in the Spirit, you can even transform your financial life, your health life, your material life, your ministry life, your spiritual life, and any other realm of life. Praying in the Spirit is one of the greatest keys, and if you will use it on a regular basis, will unlock for you the mysteries of heaven and you will tap into the fullness of life in the Spirit.

I was taught years ago that the more you pray in the Spirit, the more you will receive from the Spirit, and the more revelation you would receive, the more impartation you would receive, the more insight you would receive, the more access and opportunity to minister to others through the gifts of the Spirit would be available to you, by simply committing to dedicating yourself to praying in the Spirit or in other tongues.

Ephesians 6:10 says, "Finally my brother, be strong in the Lord and in the power of His might. Put on the whole armor of God, that you may be able to stand against the wiles of the devil." Then verse 18 says, "praying always with all prayer and supplication in the Spirit…"

One of the ways to put on the armor of God and to stand strong in the Lord, is by and through praying in the Spirit. People that don't pray in the Spirit cut themselves off from many blessings and opportunities from the Lord Jesus. Those who don't pray in the Spirit missed out on tapping into the strength of the Spirit. All they have is the natural realm in which to pray by; and they are limited in their prayer life, but when you pray in the Holy Spirit, you will tap into the unlimited power and resources of Christ.

Praying in the Spirit prepares you for your future and your destiny. As you pray in the Spirit concerning your future, the Holy Spirit begins to put it in order, and he begins to create your future and your destiny. As you pray in the Spirit, he begins to organize and put into place the necessary people needed; training and connections that you will need to fulfill God's plan and purpose for your life. As you pray in the Spirit, more than what you know, more than what you can figure out, more than what you can do in the natural begins to take place.

1 Corinthians 14:2 says, "in the Spirit he speaks mysteries…"

So as you pray in the Spirit, you are not only praying for things you have no idea of, but you are also praying and birthing supernatural mysteries. A mystery is something we don't understand fully, we can't see it yet; we have no idea about what is taking place; it's secretive and not revealed yet, and as far as you are concerned you don't even know it exists yet. As you pray in the Spirit, these things begin to unfold. These mysteries no longer remain a mystery, but you get light at the end of the tunnel. You begin to slowly understand and comprehend the plan and purpose of the Lord Jesus for your life.

All this takes place as you pray in the Spirit. There will be times when the Holy Spirit will have you pray in the Spirit for days and even weeks; sometimes even years and you have no earthly idea what you are specifically praying about. It is during this time that you are praying your future; you are prophesying your future through praying in other tongues. The Holy Spirit is having you birth all the necessary things that you will need to fulfill the plan and purpose of God, and all of this takes place as you pray in the Spirit.

1 Corinthians 14:18, "I thank my God I speak with tongues more than you all…"

Paul had a revelation of how important praying in other tongues was. He knew more about it than possibly any of us, and he did it abundantly. He boldly said he prayed this way more than anybody at that time in the body of Christ. So if the apostle Paul thought it was important, thought it was necessary to pray in tongues or in the Spirit abundantly; how much more should we be praying in the Spirit?

It is my opinion that in order to live in victory, in order to prosper and be in health, in order to continually grow in the things of the Spirit, in understanding and obeying and doing and living the Word of God; we must increase and multiply in our time of praying in the Spirit. Many things that we need to see accomplished in our life, in society, in our ministry, etc., will not be accomplished without someone spending the time and paying the price through praying in the Spirit.

Many people who are believers and love the Lord Jesus, who live holy and faithful to the Lord Jesus, have infirmities that have not yet been healed. They have strongholds that are not yet destroyed, and have bondages that they have not yet been delivered of. Their answer and breakthrough is to tap into, if they will spend the time, and if they will be committed to, is praying in the Spirit. There is an answer and I do not know what all the answers are, but this I do know; Jesus paid the price for us to be totally set free; totally and thoroughly healed and delivered, but it's up to us to press on in to him, it's up to us to press on and on to the truth, and that is only found through the person of the Holy Spirit and the revelation that he will bring to you through praying in the Spirit. Many of the answers we need in our lives, in our ministry, and in society have already been provided by the Lord Jesus, but it's up to us to press into the realm of the Spirit; to press into the realm where the Holy Spirit lives, moves, and has his being. Many of our answers that we need will not come through the realm of the natural, but they will come through the realm of the Holy Spirit and it's up to you and I to press in and as we do, he will speak the Word to you, he will manifest the word of God to you; the word that you need to hear, the word that you need to understand, the word that you need to comprehend, the word that will set you free and bring you the answers you need in your life. I find this to be true in my own life; that as I spend an abundant time praying in the Spirit, it is shortly thereafter that I receive insight, wisdom, and revelation, but if I would not have prayed in the Holy Spirit, I probably would not have received the insight, wisdom or revelation.

My wife and I are currently on a cruise in the Eastern Caribbean, and as I am receiving this from the Lord, and writing it down, there was something that came to me and that is this; for many years I declared that I believe to have received greater wisdom, insight and revelation concerning the Lord Jesus Christ; his Word and anything else that I need. It just hit me, that as I'm writing this, by inspiration of the Spirit, that prayer, that declaration is being fulfilled! Praise the Lord! But I had to stay with it even when it looked like nothing was manifesting; even when I was receiving nothing from the Lord. I just kept declaring what the Lord put in my spirit, and I just kept praying in the Holy Spirit abundantly every chance I got.

By Praying in the Spirit, you tap into the flow of the Spirit. What I mean by this, is the Holy Spirit is like a river, as he is able to flow unhindered, unrestricted, and he is able to do great and mighty things; and as you pray in the Spirit, you will tap into his divine flow; you will tap into his supernatural current which is mighty and powerful to grab hold of, all that is within you, all that is and was in the people around you and remove it. Think of a rushing mighty river; if a garbage bag is on the bank, and then the rushing mighty river grabs hold of it, it will take it off the bank of the river and downstream, and you will never see it again. The same is true with the flow of the Holy Spirit when you tap into his flow; he will take and grab the things that are in our lives, that are not of God and remove them. This all takes place through praying in the Spirit. Without praying in the Spirit none of this is possible. This tells me just how important it is to pray in the Spirit. Many changes, healings, miracles, salvation, and breakthroughs will not manifest in your life or mine, without you and I spending much time praying in the Spirit. The answers are not natural; they are spiritual, and we must receive from the Holy Spirit these answers, which are in the spiritual realm through praying in the Spirit.

Praying in the Spirit helps take you out of the flesh realm; it helps to take you out of being controlled and dominated by the works of the flesh that we find in Galatians 5:19-21, which are adultery, fornication, uncleanness, lasciviousness, idolatry, witchcraft, jealousies, hatred, outbursts of wrath, selfish ambitions, dissensions, envy, murders, drunkenness, revelries and the like.

We all have and can identify with some area of the works of the flesh that we just mentioned; that we have yet to bring under the control totally of the Holy Spirit. Praying in the Spirit will help you so that you are continually overflowing with the fullness of the Holy Spirit, and what that really means is that you are, and will be overflowing with love, joy, peace, self-control, gentleness, etc.; these manifestations of the Holy Spirit will flow out of you once they are in you in abundance, overflowing, too much. At least in part, how you get to that place, to where the fruit of the Spirit is dominating and flowing out of you, is through praying in the Spirit. Again, this is a mystery how praying in the Spirit helps you to overcome the works of the flesh; it is supernatural; you cannot overcome the flesh through the natural or through your own power. How many times have you made attempts to stop something that you are doing that was hurting you, or hurting , and yet you failed. We have all done this. One thing I know, that at least if I fail temporarily in overcoming the flesh, I can begin again, and how I do this is by praying much in the Spirit. There are times I can just sense on the inside of me as I am praying in the Spirit, that inner strength is being built up stronger and stronger as I continue to pray in other tongues. This is a work not of man, but the Holy Spirit.

Romans 8:26, "Likewise, the Spirit also helps in our weaknesses, for we do not know what we should pray for as we ought, but the Spirit Himself makes intercession for the Saints [or us] according to the will of God."

As you pray in the Spirit, Paul said the Holy Spirit would make intercession for you according to the will of God to deliver you out of all your weaknesses. He said that he would come alongside you, as you prayed in the Spirit and help you to overcome. He did not say he would do it alone; he does not do this for you, but he does this with you, as a co-labor. You pray in the Spirit, and as you pray, he comes alongside you and begins to do what only the Holy Spirit can do, and that is to help you overcome and get the victory over the works of the enemy; over the works of the flesh that the enemy is keeping you bound in, but it's as you pray in the Spirit that he comes alongside and helps you. If you do not pray in the Spirit he cannot come alongside and assist you.

If you have never been filled with the Holy Spirit and haven't received your prayer language; it is available to you as a believer in the Lord Jesus Christ! All you have to do is ask the Lord Jesus to baptize you in the Spirit and he will do it.

I received my infilling of the Spirit sitting in the last row in the Convention Center in Albuquerque, New Mexico, at a Catholic charismatic conference, and I did not even know I received it. A few days later was when my prayer language began, it wasn't instantaneous, but it did come.

My wife received her prayer language and her infilling of the Holy Spirit when she was making cookies after I prayed for her. Again, nothing happened instantaneous, but it did manifest shortly thereafter. After I prayed for her, I was heading to my mother's for a short visit, and she called me and said guess what? I got it! From that day forward until this day, we have functioned in it abundantly every day.

I do remember a time in my life when I backslid. For about three years after being born again, one of the first things that took place was that I stopped praying in the Spirit. When you stop praying in the Spirit or even back off or slowdown, you are heading for trouble; you are heading for a trap of the enemy and heading for darkness, pain and suffering. Don't fall for that deception; the deception of not praying in the Spirit. We need a proper balance of faith in the Word of God and a function of life in the Spirit. One of the ways to keep yourself properly balanced is to continue praying in the Spirit every day. Start out your day praying in the Spirit, pray in the Spirit during the course of your day as often as possible, and end your day praying in the Holy Spirit.

There is an adventure you can take every day by praying in the Spirit; it's an adventure and excitement that the natural cannot provide. As you pray in the Holy Spirit, or in other tongues, you will unlock revelation for the body of Christ that is been withheld and kept locked up until someone will hear the voice of the Lord and begin to unlock it; begin to release it into the earth through praying in the Spirit; through intercession and the birthing process of the Holy Spirit. You may not be the one who clearly sees and understands the mystery that has been locked up; but as you pray, as you birth it, as you release it into the earth through intercession, through praying in the Spirit, someone on the other side of the world may receive the insight, the wisdom and revelation of what you pray for, and now they can bring clarity and teaching of that previously hidden truth into the open all because you prayed in the Spirit, and you took the time to intercede, and the Holy Spirit through you released divine mysteries and the Holy Spirit through you brought forth fresh truth; the Holy Spirit through you brought forth fresh revelation of something that has been hidden from the body of Christ.

Matthew 13:11 he answered and said unto them, because it is given unto you to know the mysteries of the kingdom of heaven, but to them it is not given.

Jesus said here, that to you and I, the born-again, Spirit filled believer, that we are to know the mysteries of the kingdom of heaven. How we come to know the mysteries of the kingdom of heaven, is through revelation from the Holy Spirit; and that revelation is released as we pray in the Spirit and hear the voice of the Spirit, and speak what he is saying, regardless if we understand it at the time; regardless if it makes sense to us; regardless if it lines up with our theology at the moment.

When we receive revelation that has been previously hidden; it probably will not make sense and probably will not be easily accepted amongst those who are not Spirit filled. Think of the revelation that Oral Roberts received concerning healing, concerning prosperity and that God is good; he was labeled a heretic because he revealed something that was previously kept hidden; but as he kept ministering the Word of the Lord, as he kept ministering revelation, faith began to come into the hearts of the body of Christ; clarity began to come through the Word of God. As we went to school at ORU, one of the things we learned about Oral Roberts, is that he prayed in the Spirit abundantly. Before the University was even built, he walked the ground for hours upon hours praying in other tongues knowing that what God was calling him to build seemed impossible, but as he prayed, he began to birth the will of God into the earth, and so can you if you will hear the voice of the Lord; if you will pray in the Spirit abundantly and never give up, you too can birth the mysteries of heaven that have not yet been revealed in Jesus name! I remember Oral Roberts saying many times that the University and the City of Faith was built in the spiritual realm by his praying in the Spirit before any ground was taken.

If you desire to communicate the gospel with greater results and more effectively, then increase your time in praying in the Spirit!

If you desire your anointing to increase and multiply, not only do you need to declare that with your faith that your anointing is increasing and multiplying, but you also need to increase and multiply in praying in the Spirit; as you increase and multiply in praying in the Spirit, you tap into the fullness of Luke 4:18 which says the Spirit of the Lord is upon me and has anointed me to preach the gospel to the poor; he has anointed me to bring deliverance to the bound, he has anointed me to open blind eyes…

In acts 10:38 how God anointed Jesus of Nazareth with the Holy Spirit and with power who went about doing good and healing all those that were oppressed of the devil…

2 Corinthians 2:4 and my speech and my preaching were not with persuasive words of

human wisdom, but in demonstration of the Spirit and of power…

Notice the apostle Paul said his preaching was filled with supernatural power; also remember that the apostle Paul said he prayed in tongues more than anybody in the body of Christ at that time.

Praying in the Spirit is the key that causes your anointing to increase and multiply. The more you pray in the Spirit, the more your anointing will increase and multiply with supernatural power to save the lost, to heal the sick, to raise the dead, to deliver the bound, to open the eyes of the natural and spiritually blind. All of this cannot be done through natural means; it takes spiritual power of the Holy Spirit to do this, and we must do whatever it takes to tap into that power and get it flowing in our midst.

The more you pray in the Spirit the more you will flow with the Holy Spirit.

If you have difficulty with temptation in some area of your life, pray in the Spirit to the degree and into the depth that the Holy Spirit is calling you to, and you will find that temptation decreasing more and more every day, but the key is praying in the Spirit until the Holy Spirit releases you.

A person that prays much in the Holy Spirit will be a person that will recognize and discern the lies and temptations of the enemy. A person that prays much in the Holy Spirit will be a person of overcoming victory. If you are a teenager, one of the easiest ways to defeat peer pressure is to pray much in the Holy Spirit. The more victories you want, the more wisdom you want, the more anointing you want, the more of the gifts of the Holy Spirit you want will require you to pray much in the Spirit.

Many of us pray just enough to survive, but there is much more to prayer and intercession than just survival praying; there is what I call overcoming victorious praying which includes declaring much of what God's Word says about victory, as well as praying much in the Holy Spirit. The more you want, the more you need to pray in the Spirit. If you are satisfied and enjoy struggle, barely surviving both spiritually and naturally; then just keep on praying on the level you are currently praying, which probably is just enough to survive.

Think of it this way; you can eat food and drink water just enough to stay alive, but eventually it will catch up with you and you will begin to suffer in your body. The same is true concerning spiritual things, concerning praying in the Holy Spirit. We need to go to the realm of overcoming victory; we need to go to the realm of abundance in regards to praying in the Holy Spirit.

People that are weak spiritually; people that are carnal instead of being spiritually minded, are people that either don't pray in the spirit at all, or they pray very little in the Spirit. Which one are you? Are you weak? Are you carnal? Or are you a man or woman of God that has decided that you want overcoming victory in every area of your life? If you want overcoming victory in every area of your life, it will require you to pray in the Holy Spirit unto the realm of victory. It will require you to pray in the Holy Spirit as he leads you further and further into the realm of the Spirit, and into victory. You will be required to pray in the Holy Spirit until on the inside, you know that your prayer assignment is completed.

When you pray in the Spirit you will build a supernatural hedge of divine protection that is promised to you in Psalm 91; all around you and all around your family, and all around your ministry, and all around your city and nation. Many who have an apostolic anointing are intercessors, and when they pray much in the Spirit, they will build a supernatural hedge of protection over their assigned territory. I remember when hurricane Charley was headed towards Fort Myers Beach, Florida, for many weeks previous to this, we spent much time on the beach enjoying the beach and fasting and praying as we were at the beach. When the hurricane was approaching our city, we were declaring Psalm 91 over Fort Myers Beach; that the Lord Jesus had assigned his angels to that beach and that no evil could come near that beach. We also spent much time praying in the Holy Spirit against that storm, and the meteorologist said that the eye of the hurricane was headed to Fort Myers Beach, but it looked like it hit a wall and bounced back out into the ocean, and it went further up the coast until it found a place that it could enter. I am convinced that if other people would've been assigned further up the coast to intercede and to do battle for that part of the beach, it would not have entered. There is a good realm of possibility that the Holy Spirit called other people to that area to pray, and either they did not obey, or they did not pray accurately or they did not pray to the depths that the Holy Spirit needed them to pray, to war off the hurricane that was approaching. How many times do natural storms bring destruction, and it is not God's will for any community or individual to be destroyed through storms whether their natural or spiritual, but it takes a man or woman of God to rise up and to hear the call of God and do battle in the realm of the spirit, by the power of the Holy Spirit; and much of this is done through praying in the Holy Spirit or through praying in tongues.

Do you want to bring change and divine protection to your community? Then you must answer the call of God to pray in the Holy Spirit strongly, faithfully and boldly. You must pray in the Holy Spirit until your assignment is completed. Some assignments are quick and some assignments take years to get fulfilled, but we must remain faithful; we must remain diligent and never back off praying in the Holy Spirit!

Praying in the Holy Spirit takes faith. Your mind and emotions have no idea what is going on, and they will war against you to try to keep you from doing what God wants you to do. They will war against you and try to fill you with doubt and unbelief; they will try to get you off your prayer assignment, but you must persevere, you must battle through, you must remain faithful and keep on praying in the Holy Spirit until your prayer assignment is fulfilled. Religious people do not understand this type of praying; they cannot enter into it because it takes the Holy Spirit to lead you into it, and religious people are more naturally minded than Holy Spirit led. That's why Paul said in 2 Corinthians 2:9-14 the eye has not seen, nor ear heard, nor have entered into the heart of man, the things which God has prepared for those who love him; but God has revealed them to us through his Spirit. For the Holy Spirit searches all things, yes the deep things of God... The natural man does not receive the things of the Spirit of God, for they are foolishness to him; nor can he know them, because they are spiritually discerned.

A person who does not pray in the Holy Spirit and led by the Holy Spirit, will be a person who is more natural minded than spiritually minded. The things of the Holy Spirit will be foolishness to a religious person, but nonetheless, to a spiritually Holy Spirit minded and led type of person; they are life; they are instructions, and they are a blessing. This type of person prays much in the Holy Spirit. Also a note of caution; religious minded people that you share spiritual truths with cannot understand them, and they will think you are flaky; they will think you are weird. It is better to keep them to yourself than to share them with a religious person. That's why Jesus said:

Matthew 7:6 give not that which is holy unto the dogs, neither cast your pearls before swine…

Casting your pearls before swine is sharing Holy Spirit revelation with naturally minded carnal Christians who spend very little or no time at all praying in the Holy Spirit. If you try to do this, you are giving that which is holy unto dogs. I did not call anybody a dog, that is just a term that in Bible days referred to the Gentiles or an unbeliever; and if that is you, you can call upon the Lord Jesus and he will save you and fill you with his Holy Spirit, and transform you out of being carnal into being filled with his Holy Spirit, overflowing with his Holy Spirit bringing life, and that life more abundantly to those around you; to those that will accept the Lord Jesus Christ as Lord and Savior.

So it takes faith to please God (see Hebrews 11:6). It takes faith to answer the call to life in the Spirit. It takes faith to hear the call of God and what God's word says and to obey it; be faithful to it. It takes faith to walk in the fullness of the Holy Spirit, and to pray in the fullness of the Holy Spirit. Praying in the fullness of the Holy Spirit is not for the weak timid Christians. It's for the warrior; it's for the man or woman of God who hungers and thirsts for heaven on earth. It is for the man or woman of God who wants to exalt the Lord Jesus Christ, and be all that he created us to be. Every time you begin to pray in the Spirit, your faith is being released; your faith is being activated to go into a realm that you have never gone before. Your faith is being released and activated to accomplish a specific purpose in the mind of Christ, and as you pray in the Holy Spirit you will tap into the mind of Christ and birth what is on his mind into the earth.

Galatians 4:19 My little children, for whom I labor and birth again until Christ is formed in you.

Remember Christ means the anointing and the anointed one. Paul says that he will enter into a realm of labor and birthing until the anointing and the anointed one is created and increased in your life, and this is done through praying in the Holy Spirit. This is one of the foundational scriptures the Lord has given me for the work we are doing here in Florida, and we will accomplish our assignment as we continue to battle through and pray much in and through the Holy Spirit.

Praying in the Holy Spirit takes boldness, strength and fervency. In order to pray in the Spirit, you have to have the boldness of Proverbs 28:1 the righteous are as bold as a lion. Jesus is referred to as the lion of the tribe of Judah, and you need to learn to roar through the Holy Spirit, and you will do this as you pray in the Spirit. When you pray in the Spirit, there is a sound that comes out of you; that to the kingdom of darkness it sounds like an angry ferocious hungry lion that is on the attack, and just like in the natural when you hear a lion approaching and roaring, you will flea in terror thinking you're about to be destroyed. That is what happens when you pray in the Holy Spirit through a spirit of boldness and you put on the lion of the tribe of Judah. It takes strength from another dimension to pray this way, and all of this is available to you as you pray in other tongues abundantly.

Jeremiah 25:30 the Lord will roar from on high, and uttered his voice from his habitation; he will roar mightily...

Amos 1:2 the Lord roars from Zion, and utters his voice from Jerusalem...

So there is a Holy Spirit roar that comes out of you when you pray in the Holy Spirit and tap into the lion of the tribe of Judah who is the Lord Jesus Christ. As you yield yourself to the Holy Spirit, the roar of the lion of the tribe of Judah begins to flow out of you, begins to be sounded through you into all the earth, into the realm of the Spirit and against all the workers of darkness which are the demonic, and the demonic people that are yielded to the demonic.

Most people, if not all people that will pray with the roar of the lion of the tribe of Judah, will be people that are prophetic in nature that have a prophetic anointing. The sound of the roar of the lion of the tribe of Judah comes through the prophets and the prophetic people. Notice two of the references concerning the roar of the Lord were revealed through the prophet Jeremiah and the prophet Amos. So, if you have a prophetic anointing, get ready to roar, get ready to yield yourself greater and greater to the lion of the tribe of Judah so he can roar in the earth. There is a greater roar coming. There is a roar that's going to come through prophetic praise and through the instruments of the Psalmists, and musicians will yield themselves to the Holy Spirit and to the lion of the tribe of Judah. How you do this at least in part, is by praying much in the Holy Spirit. When no one can see you. Most people that do this are humble people, they are people not looking for recognition, they just want to fulfill the call of God upon their life; they just want to please the Lord Jesus Christ and it takes great faith in order to do this.

Praying in the Holy Spirit will tap you into the realm where God lives so you can hear him more clearly, be encouraged by him, and be empowered by him. It also helps you to stay yielded to him; to stay yielded to his purpose and plan for your life.

Praying in the Holy Spirit prepares the way of the Lord. Is there some way, some path that you need opened, that you need revealed, that you need cleared of debris; of things that may keep you from his plan and purpose? All these things will be accomplished as you pray in the Holy Spirit. The way of the Lord will be revealed as you as you pray in the Holy Spirit. It may not happen today, it might not happen by next week, but it will come to pass as you keep praying in the Holy Spirit. He will prepare the way of the Lord. That's what it means to prepare the way of the Lord. To prepare a way for the Lord Jesus and his plan and purpose to be fulfilled in you, and in all the earth. He will make the way clear, he will reveal the way as you pray in the Holy Spirit!

Mark 1:2-3 as it is written in the prophets, behold I will send my messenger before your face who will prepare your way before you. The voice of one crying in the wilderness prepare the way of the Lord may see his paths straight.

John the Baptist had to prepare the way of the Lord for the Lord Jesus to come into the earth. He came before Jesus in ministry, ministering what saith the Lord, and by doing this, he prepared a path; he cleared a way for the Lord Jesus to come. In like manner we do the same thing through praying in the Holy Spirit; we prepare a path for the Lord Jesus to come into people's lives, into situations and circumstances, into nations so they can hear clearly the Gospel of the Lord Jesus Christ and the word of the Lord. This is all done through men and women of God who will pray much in the Holy Spirit as well as the men and women of God who speak the word of the Lord, both are necessary, both are important.

The more you pray in the Holy Spirit, the more prepared you will be for the move of the Spirit and for a fresh outpouring of the Holy Spirit.

Acts 1:4 and being assembled together with them, he commanded them not to depart from Jerusalem, but to wait for the promise of the Father, which he said, you shall be baptized with the Holy Spirit not many days from now.

In verse 12-14 and when they had entered they went up into the upper room… These all continued with one accord in prayer and supplication…

Before they could experience the fresh move of the Holy Spirit, they had to be prepared. I know at this moment in time, they were not able to pray in the Spirit, but I am convinced that as they gathered together and prayed in the natural realm they were preparing for what would be experienced for thousands of years to come, and that is a continual fresh outpouring of the Holy Spirit. In every move of God one thing is for certain; there is much praying in the Holy Spirit. As you pray in the Holy Spirit you are being prepared and you are preparing others for a fresh wind of the Spirit of God for a fresh outpouring of the Holy Spirit.

As you pray in the Spirit you will put on your spirit man; the armor that is referred to in Ephesians 6:10-18. The more you pray in the Spirit, the sharper your sword of the Spirit is. The more you pray in the spirit, the more the Word of God becomes alive to you; becomes activated in you; becomes more than just a religious book that you have to read or listen to sermons from; the Word of God becomes alive to you, and you hunger to hear that clear, uncompromised word of God, not a word that is watered down with excuses, but one that is filled with power to change lives and to perform signs, wonders and miracles. All this is done as you pray in the Holy Spirit.

Praying in the Holy Spirit is a weapon of offense against your enemy. The more you pray in the Holy Spirit, the more you will be on the offense inside of things and not the defensive side of things. Have you ever noticed how many people are responding to what the enemy does to them instead of making the enemy respond to their attacks on offense? I am a Green Bay Packer fan, and we have a powerful offense; one that can score quickly, one that puts fear in the hearts of the defense not knowing if they will score quickly through a long pass; through a short pass, or through a run by one of the running backs. A strong offense is a powerful weapon; you and I can have that strong offense as we pray in the Holy Spirit abundantly, not just enough to survive. We will pray in the Holy Spirit like a warrior, as an athlete boldly, fervently and

aggressively exercises and works out, we will do the same thing through praying in the Spirit.

As you pray in the Spirit, you will tap into all that Jesus is, and all that he has provided for us on the cross of Calvary. As you pray in the Spirit, you will tap into and receive the full inheritance that he came to give you. It's just not enough to claim it by faith. It's just not enough to speak the Word of God, but you need to combine it with fervent bold prayer of the Holy Spirit, which is other tongues.

Praying in the Holy Spirit is not something you can just wait for God to do for you; it is something you just have to step out in faith and begin to do as the Holy Spirit leads you. Just like in Matthew 14 when Peter stepped out of the boat, he stepped out of the natural realm and he began to walk on the water to go to Jesus just because Jesus said come. Notice that Peter had to inquire of the Lord; Jesus did not say to all of them to come, only the one that required a word from him, and when that word came, he stepped out of the boat and began to walk upon the water which is something that is supernatural; it is not normal to walk on water. It takes the power of the Holy Spirit to walk on water. So if you're waiting for God to do it, or for God to make you do it, he's not going to; you are going to have to step out in faith and ask him for the fullness of the Holy Spirit and then just began the flow as the Holy Spirit leads you; just open your mouth and he will fill it with a heavenly prayer language!

When you are a babe in Christ, you might've been able to pray in the Holy Spirit say 30 minutes a day and that was sufficient for you to live a life of faith and holiness, but as you began to grow older in the Lord Jesus and as you begin to mature, he will call you deeper, but if you do not respond to him by praying more in the Holy Spirit; then the amount of praying in the Holy Spirit you did as a babe in Christ will not accomplish for you what it used to, and that is because 30 minutes is not enough for you today, 60 minutes may not be enough; for some eight hours may not be enough; it's all according to the call of God upon your life and to what you want to accomplish spiritually in this earth, and what he wants to accomplish through you in this earth; that will all depend on how much you pray in the Holy Spirit. The more you want to accomplish and the more he wants to accomplish through you, will require of you much prayer in the Holy Spirit.

Praying in the Holy Spirit opens the door to the supernatural. It prepares you and makes you available to all the manifestations of the Holy Spirit found in I Corinthians chapter 12. As you study on the gifts of the Holy Spirit, and as you study on each specific gift and then make yourself available to the Holy Spirit, by simply saying, Holy Spirit I make myself available to you and to the gift of the working of miracles and to the gifts of healing so on and so forth. As you do this, you will be prepared when the Holy Spirit moves upon you to step out in faith and let him flow through you in ministering life to another. The Holy Spirit is a gentleman and he will not force himself upon you; he will not force you to do anything you don't want to do, and that is why we need to make ourselves available to the Holy Spirit and to each specific gifting of the Holy Spirit; then pray in other tongues for as long as is necessary. Most of the gifts of the Holy Spirit that operates through you today, operate through you today because of the praying and study of God's Word you did previously. So, if you want more of the gifts of the Holy Spirit to manifest through you; you need to pray greater and greater in the Spirit.

I Corinthians 12:7: "The manifestation of the Spirit is given to every man severally as He wills."

As Novel Hayes once said, the Holy Spirit is always willing to give his gifts to a yielded vessel, so you can expect the Holy Spirit to give you all his gifts.

One thing I learned years ago, is that if I have the fullness of the Holy Spirit living in me, then I have all of his gifts available to me and it's up to me to tap into them; it's up to me to call them forth in Jesus name, it's up to me to be prepared, and it's only up to him when and how they will manifest, but the rest is my responsibility.

As you pray in the Spirit, you are being refilled with the Holy Spirit. This is why it's so important to pray every day in other tongues, because when you do, your level of the infilling of the Holy Spirit increases as you pray.

As you pray in the Holy Spirit, it is just the beginning of tapping into the prophetic side of Christ. I have never met anybody with a prophetic anointing that has not been Spirit filled and prayed much in the Spirit. You cannot prophesy without being Spirit filled. I also have never met someone with a prophetic anointing who does not pray much in other tongues. So if you do not pray in the Holy Spirit, you can never tap into the prophetic side of Jesus Christ; it's impossible.

As you pray in the Spirit, you are plowing up the ground in your life that needs to be plowed up. Mark chapter 4:14-20 speaks of the different types of ground that our hearts are; one of those grounds is a hard heart, or through the difficulties of life, our soil, our ground, becomes hardened through disappointments and wounds in our soul, so we need at times to plow it up and as you pray in other tongues you will plow up that soil.

There are other areas that also need to be plowed up, and that is the areas where you need to grow in; that is areas that you need to take for the gospel of the kingdom too, that is areas that the enemy has had under his control and domination and it needs to be plowed up and you do this by praying in the Holy Spirit.

Jeremiah 26:18 "Zion shall be plowed …"

Hosea 10: 11 "Judah shall plow…"

Spiritual plowing just like natural plowing is not a lot of fun. Spiritual plowing is hard work. Spiritual plowing is done through the prophetic anointing; prophets plow. When a prophet prays, when someone with a prophetic anointing prays, they will almost always begin plowing in the realm of the Spirit in the area they are assigned to pray, whether it's spiritual, financial, or things in the natural realm that need to be changed. In order to accomplish this assignment, you need to plow in the realm of the spirit through the anointing of the Holy Spirit by praying in the Spirit.

When plowing, you have to be focused on the end result; you have to be determined with a Holy Spirit determination not to quit when it gets difficult, because like I said, plowing is hard work and it takes great faith to plow just like it takes a farmer great vision, strength, and refusing to give up after the long, hard, hot days of plowing out in the sun in the summertime. That's what we do when we pray in the Holy Spirit. That's what we do as plowman of the Spirit.

Amos 9:13: "Behold the days are coming declares the Lord when the plowman shall overtake the reader and the treader of grapes him who sows the seed…"

There is a day coming that the Lord promises and has prophesied that you shall reap almost immediately after you plowed the field and sow the seed. It will be so that as soon as you sow you shall reap.

One thing many have not yet seen or understood and have not done, is plow the ground before we plant the seed; and what that means, is that before you can minister the Word of God to an individual , or before you minister the Word of God to a church, or to a city, or to a nation; the soil must be plowed. How you do that is through intercession, and by praying in the Holy Spirit or in tongues. We all want an awesome harvest of the seed we sow; but remember, the ground has to be plowed before the seed can be sown and before you can reap a harvest; so I challenge you to launch out in faith and become a plowman of the Spirit; plow those areas that have never been plowed before; hear the voice of the Holy Spirit calling you to those areas that have never been plowed before and begin plowing by the anointing of the Holy Spirit, by the power of the Holy Spirit. God wants us to be the prophetic people he has called us to be and to plow where no one has plowed before. Also, there are grounds that are only half plowed and they need to be finished before the seed can be sown and before a harvest can be reaped. Someone may have begun plowing that field and for whatever reason was not able to complete the task at hand, whether it was the Lord telling them to stop or it was just too difficult at that time to accomplish the task at hand. Nevertheless, it's got to be finished. There is no condemnation if you started plowing and stopped; the important thing is to begin again and to complete the task at hand. So be encouraged and be strengthened by the power of the Holy Spirit in Jesus name, and go forth and be the plowman that God has called you to be!

Romans 8:1 "There is now therefore no condemnation to those who are in Christ Jesus…"

Praying in the Holy Spirit binds the works of darkness and destroys Satan's evil strategies against your life, against your church, against

your city, against your family and against your life.

Matthew 16:19 I will give you the keys of the kingdom of heaven and whatever you bind on earth shall be bound in heaven, and whatever you loose on earth shall be loosed in heaven.

Praying in the Holy Spirit is one of the ways you can bind and loose in. As you pray in the Holy Spirit or in other tongues, the Holy Spirit begins to go to work to binding the forces of darkness and to loosen the kingdom of God into the earth.

As you pray in the Holy Spirit, you will also loosen your ministering angels to stay on assignment and to complete the task at hand. As you continue to pray in other tongues they continue battling; they continue working on your behalf to bring to pass the Word of God that you have confessed; to bring to pass the Word of God that you have decreed, and to bring to pass that which you are praying about in other tongues. You may not have any comprehension of what you are praying about, but the Holy Spirit does and he will direct the angels on what needs to be done because of what you are praying about.

Hebrews 1:14 are they not all ministering spirits sent out to serve for the sake of those Lord to inherit salvation?

Our angels serve us, minister to us, work in the realm of the Spirit where we cannot see in the natural, but we can know that they are at work on our behalf.

There is so much that goes on in the realm of the Spirit when we pray in the Holy Spirit that is mind-boggling, it is supernatural, it is awesome!

Praying in the Holy Spirit brings the light of God to shine on the path he is calling you to walk on. Praying in the Holy Spirit releases the light, releases the life, releases hope, releases faith, releases soundness in every area of our life. All this takes place as you pray in the Spirit.

People who are not Spirit filled even though they pray daily and have a relationship with the Lord Jesus, very seldom if ever, have supernatural miracles, supernatural healings, supernatural restoration, supernatural deliverances in their lives and ministries. All of what I just described functions through the anointing and the infilling of the Holy Spirit found in Acts chapter 2:1-4.

Acts 19:1-6 and it happened while Apollo was at Corinth; Paul passed through the inland country and came to Ephesus. There he found some disciples and he said to them, did you receive the Holy Spirit when you believe? And I said, no, we have not even heard that there is

a Holy Spirit... And they began speaking in tongues and prophesying.

So we see here that these were believers in the Lord Jesus Christ, and yet they never received the infilling of the Holy Spirit. When Paul laid his hands upon them and imparted into them the infilling of the Holy Spirit, they immediately did two things. First they spoke in other tongues and they prophesied. Until this time, they neither prayed in other tongues nor prophesied; so we conclude from this that it takes the infilling of the Holy Spirit to pray in the Spirit and it takes the infilling of the Holy Spirit to prophesy or to do any other manifestation of the Holy Spirit found in Ist Corinthians chapter 12. If you want the manifestations of the Holy Spirit in your life and to flow through your life to others, you need to first be filled with the Holy Spirit and when you are, a short time later your prayer language, your ability to pray in the Holy Spirit or in other tongues will manifest. And as you pray in the Holy Spirit, you will release supernatural power into the direction, into the assignment for which you are praying for, without the infilling of the Holy Spirit all you have is in the natural, and that always comes up way short. Think about medical science; they can do much and it is awesome what they can do, but they still cannot do everything.

They cannot put a limb back when it has been removed, but God can. They cannot give you new blood or a new DNA, but God can. They cannot give you new organs without any complications, but God can. That is because our God is a supernatural, healing, delivering and loving God! This all takes place as you train in the Spirit. You may not even realize it, but as you pray in the Spirit, someone on the other side of the country or in another nation, receives a miracle all because you prayed in the Spirit.

I pray much in the Spirit; if I had to put a number on it, it could be a minimum of two hours a day, and some days I pray much more than that. This message, this revelation is igniting me to pray more than that; if I did not have to work a natural job, I literally could pray hours upon hours as a Holy Spirit leads me. This is my desire; to not only pastor, to not only function prophetically and apostolically, but to be the intercessor that I have always been from the day I got born again; that was my first calling, it is my first love and I know that prayer changes everything, because I have experienced living as a drug addict totally lost, and yet my mother never gave up on me; she constantly prayed for me and at the right moment the Holy Spirit broke through and transformed my life out of darkness into light. So being a prayer warrior, an intercessor burns within me to pray for those that are in darkness, to pray for those that are hurting, to pray for those that are bound, to pray for the church of the Lord Jesus Christ to be awakened, to be revived, to be diligent, to be on fire and to fulfill the call of God upon our life. None of this can take place without praying in the Spirit. The more we pray in the Holy Spirit, the more we will accomplish our assignments in Jesus name!

Praying in the Holy Spirit is a must if you want to deal with the demonic victoriously.

Luke 9:1 and he called the twelve together and gave them power and authority over all demons…

Luke 10:17 Lord, even the demons are subject to us in your name.

We know we are called to deal with the demonic as Spirit filled believers, but in order to deal with them victoriously, we must be built up in our inner man according to Jude verse 20 which says; beloved building yourselves up in your most holy faith praying in the Holy Spirit. So, we see here that in order to cast out demons and to live in victory over the demonic, our inner man must be built- up, and our inner man must be strengthened with the might of the Holy Spirit.

Ephesians 3:16 that according to the riches of his glory that he might grant you to be strengthened with power through his Spirit in your inner being…

When we pray in the Holy Spirit we build our inner man up so that our inner man is like the lion of the tribe of Judah when it comes to dealing with the demonic, and it attacks and destroys the works of the enemy. You cannot deal with the demonic if your spirit is weak; if you have not spent time strengthening your spirit through praying in the Holy Spirit. If you are dealing with demonic things, have not yet gotten the victory over them, I would encourage you to increase and even double the amount of time you pray in the Holy Spirit and you will see victory come forth, because as you pray the lion of the tribe of Judah through the person of the Holy Spirit, and through the power of the Spirit you will conquer the demonic and you will get the victory, but you need to do your part which is pray in the Holy Spirit and confess God's Word; decree what God's Word says about your situation and do not back down. Defeat is not an option for the Spirit filled believer!

We have many strongholds we in our minds, in our emotions, in our mental state of being, or in any other area of life; many of them if not all of them, are demonic. The demonic is behind them, and in order to get the victory over them and to see those strongholds demolished, we must pray with a greater revelation of praying in the Spirit, and we must pray from and into greater power of the Spirit!

2 Corinthians 10:3-5 for though we walk in the flesh, we are not waging war according to the flesh. For the weapons of our warfare are not of the flesh, but have divine power to destroy strongholds. We destroy arguments and every lofty opinion raised against the knowledge of God and take every thought captive to obey Christ…

It takes spiritual weapons to destroy strongholds; it takes spiritual weapons to destroy demonic thoughts, and it takes spiritual weapons to destroy the lies and deceptions of the enemy. One of the mightiest weapons that you have is your prayer language and when you pray in the Holy Spirit, the Holy Spirit and the angels of God go forth in battle to do whatever is necessary for you to be victorious and set free, but it takes you spending the time praying in the Spirit in order to receive that victory.

Praying in the Holy Spirit puts spiritual pressure like a volcano upon the demonic and they know an eruption is close; so they flee in terror knowing that the power of God is about to hit them and destroy them. That's why many times when you are praying in the Holy Spirit, there will be a building up inside of you like a volcano, and when you pray long enough and hard enough, then an eruption will take place, and you will have the victory.

As you pray in the Holy Spirit, the forces of darkness are pushed back. They are pushed away from you and from your situations, and from your circumstances all because you pray in and through the power of the Holy Spirit.

Praying in the Holy Spirit ignites your faith and keeps you functioning in the highest level of faith possible. If you want to have faith that moves mountains according to Mark 11:23, you need to pray abundantly in the Holy Spirit and as you do, when it's time to release your faith against the mountain, it will be released like dynamite with a supernatural explosion, which will result in moving your mountain out of the way.

Little praying in the Holy Spirit= little feeding on God's word= little results of God's Word. So ask yourself this question, is my faith functioning at its highest level? Is my faith strong enough to move the mountains I need moved?

There are two ingredients that make up strong faith; the first is spending an abundant time feeding upon God's Word. The second is praying abundantly in the Holy Spirit. If you do these two things your faith will begin to function at its highest level. It may not be today, it may not be next week, or even next month, but at some point in time as you pray in the Spirit and feed abundantly upon God's Word, your faith will begin to soar; your faith will begin to move mountains that you never thought possible; your faith will be released like dynamite; like a volcano that is ready to be erupted with Holy Spirit power. But again, it's up to you and me to spend quality time in God's Word and in praying in the Holy Spirit.

The greater the mountain, the greater you'll need to spend in God's Word and in praying in the Holy Spirit. So if the amount of time you have been spending in God's Word, and in praying in the Holy Spirit has not been sufficient to move the mountain, it's time to increase your time in God's Word and in praying in the Holy Spirit. It may also be time to get connected with some other prayer warriors to stand with you in intercession, in spiritual battle and in faith to help you move the mountain.

Also the greater you're calling is, the greater your mission in life is, the greater the assignment is, the greater you must pray in the Holy Spirit.

How many people are you called to minister to? How many cities are you called to minister to? How many cities are you called to go into to minister to? That will be dependent upon how much you yield to praying in the Holy Spirit, for that is the key to reaching the world for Christ, because it takes his power to reach them, it takes miracles, signs and wonders to reach them. Praying in the Holy Spirit launches you like a rocket into this realm. Think about how a spaceship is released into orbit, it has to be launched, and so it is with the kingdom of God that you and I have to be launched into ministry to reach the nations, and the way we do this is to pray and much in the Holy Spirit.

Praying in the Holy Spirit will bring you into the shalom of Christ; the supernatural rest that can only come through being in Christ's presence. As you pray in the Holy Spirit, you will be launched into the supernatural realm of rest.

Hebrews 4:11 let us labor therefore to enter into that rest…

Isaiah 28:11-12 for with stammering lips and another time will he speak to this people. To whom he said this is the rest wherewith you may cause the weary to rest; and this is the refreshing…

So we see here that there is a supernatural rest, a supernatural peace, a supernatural refreshing that takes place in our lives when we pray in the Holy Spirit, but there is a laboring of the Spirit, and that laboring is you and I praying in the Holy Spirit. When we pray in the Holy Spirit we tap into the shalom that comes from Jesus Christ; remember what the word shalom means; it means wholeness, soundness, completeness, nothing missing and nothing broken, it also means peace and rest. When you pray in the Holy Spirit you tap into these dimensions of the Lord Jesus Christ, you tap into who he is and he is the Prince of peace, and if you want in the abundance of peace in your life, if you want an abundance of peace in your circumstances and situations, if you want to stop laboring so much in the natural then increase your time praying in the Holy Spirit. As you do, the Holy Spirit will go to work inside of you, the Holy Spirit will go to work in your situations and circumstances, and begin to flood you with a supernatural rest, and he will begin to flood you with a supernatural peace. It is awesome to be at peace and to be in a state of rest when you face difficult circumstances, and this can come if you spend

the time in prayer by praying in the Holy Spirit.

All the things we've learned concerning confessing God's Word, concerning decreeing God's Word, concerning feeding on God's Word is a must and it can never be aborted, but we must see that it is just as important to spend quality time praying in the Holy Spirit. We need both of these ingredients to have a victorious successful life and ministry. You can't just have one or the other, but both are a necessity. If you are majoring in one or the

other, it's time to be properly balanced with both of them.

Proverbs 11:1 a false balance is abomination to the Lord: but a just weight is his delight.

Or you could say it this way; when we are properly balanced with the Word of God and the Holy Spirit, we bring the Lord Jesus great delight in great praise.

Proverbs 16:11 a just weight and balance are the Lords…

He wants us to be properly balanced with the Word of God and life in the Spirit.

Praying in the Holy Spirit will help you find your place in the kingdom and the wisdom to function in it. It will also help you when you're faced with should I or should I not do something, should I or should I not go somewhere, or should I or should I not buy this; praying in the Holy Spirit will help you with those decisions.

Praying in the Holy Spirit brings you into the things God has prepared for you from the foundation of the world, and as you pray those things will be revealed.

2 Corinthians 2:9-10 what no eye has seen, nor ear heard, nor the heart of man imagined what God has prepared for those who love him, but these things God has revealed to us through his Spirit. For the Spirit searches everything, even the depths of God…

There are things that the Holy Spirit has been sent to you to reveal to you about what God has planned for you in your life. It is beyond what you could think or ask. It will always be amazing, and there's no way that you couldn't even imagine the type of life he has for you, it is abundant, it is supernatural. The only way to tap into it is with your faith and by praying in the Holy Spirit and as you do the Holy Spirit will begin to reveal it to you; he will send prophets to prophesy it to you. He will give you dreams and supernatural visions concerning the great plans he has for you, and all this will come to pass as you pray in the Holy Spirit, as you birth his plans and purposes for your life into the earth. Actually, as you pray in the Holy Spirit, the Holy Spirit births through you his plans and purposes that are in God's heart.

This revelation is not just about information, but it is about taking what you learn and then applying it, doing it. Many can pray in the Spirit, many know of some of the reasons they should pray in the Spirit, and yet they do not pray like they should in the Spirit. So it's not just about a teaching, but it is about God calling you and me to wake up to the greatness of praying in the Spirit and then do it every day in Jesus name!

I pray that you would be ignited for a greater life in the Spirit and then go for it with all the fire and faith Jesus has deposited within you in Jesus name!

Chapter 2

In conclusion, I have one more word from the Lord to encourage us to ignite us to pray in the Holy Spirit as often as possible.

In Luke chapter 5 Jesus said to launch out into the deep….

Those that are living life in shallow waters, it's now time to come into the deep. I call those in the shallow waters to come out of the shallow and run and launch into the depth of praying in the Spirit in Jesus name! As I am speaking this, I am picturing a teenager, or a child running off the edge of the peer to jump into a lake; he has no fears, he has no hesitation, he has no concerns, he is just launching out into the deep because he knows in the deep is where the fun is and so it is in the realm of the Spirit, you have to be in the deep in order to see the signs, wonders and miracles that Jesus has for us. Those living in the shallow waters are living where it's comfortable, where it's known, but it's now time to rise up and press into the unknown journey of the Spirit into the deep.

Fear and unbelief has kept the church bound in shallow waters, but faith is here if you will take it and launch out into the deep.

I declare that the chains, the doubts, the unbelief that has kept The church in shallow waters is now broken in Jesus name!

When you get out into the deep waters, don't panic, don't fear, just rest in the Lord and float and swim in the deep waters. If you panic you will drown, but if you rest, float, and swim, you will enjoy life in deep waters. Don't look for the ground of comfort, but look to thrive in the deep waters! Most people that drown in deep waters, both in the natural and in the spiritual, do so because they panic, because they get in fear for their life. How many people panic when trouble comes, they stopped praying in the Spirit and they allow unbelief and doubt to oppress them, they lose their shout, their joy, their victory, they stopped or backed off, and they only do what makes them feel comfortable. When we do that, we retreat to shallow water, to the known, to what they can see, feel, touch etc., praying in the Holy Spirit presses you into the unknown; it is unknown in the natural, but not in the spiritual.

Hebrews 11:8 Reveals Abraham did not know in the natural where he was going, but he knew in the Spirit realm that it is the place God was building; it was a promised land and he knew that when he got there he was in his their place.

Don't live in shallow waters, don't let fear chain you; fear binds you to a life of shallow water living, but get rid of fear and launch out into the deep as the Holy Spirit of God leads you there one step at a time.

Don't be focused on being comfortable; always remember faith steps out, it does not need to know the end result, it just hears and obeys the voice of the Spirit of God.

Your days of being allowed to remain in the shallow waters are over; you will have no grace to live in the shallow waters says the Lord . If you remain in the shallow waters, you will be miserable, unhappy, and defeated, because you continued in shallow waters; but as you step out of the shallow waters you will experience joy, victory, fulfillment even though things could be quite challenging for a season.

Everything we are, every revelation, every impartation, every anointing is linked to your prayer life. Your prayer life is the foundation on which your life spiritually and naturally is built. There is no formula to follow, it's just simply to start praying in the Holy Spirit, and as you pray the Holy Spirit will lead you into greater depths of prayer which will strengthen your inner man, which will strengthen your foundation which we know has to be the Word of God, which will give you greater victory, greater revelation and greater miracles. As you pray in the Holy Spirit, you can expect greater manifestations of the Holy Spirit, greater manifestations of his gifts, of his fruit, of his power, anointing and glory. You can expect a deeper walk with Jesus in knowing him, in loving him, in being faithful to him, and obey him. You can inspect every part of your spiritual life and your natural life to grow increase and multiply. You can expect greater dreams, greater visions, greater Holy Spirit experiences, and most of all a greater reaching of souls for the kingdom of God!

Every believer prays on some level and it's time for us all to go deeper in praying in the Holy Spirit!

Just think about it in the book of Acts chapter 2; the church was birthed as they prayed in the Spirit. All the salvations and miracles we read about were all directly related to their ability to be a people of prayer. What would've happened if they had not remained in the upper room and received the baptism of the Holy Spirit? They probably would've been much like the church today, void of power but full of excuses and religion. So we need to pray in the Holy Spirit and don't stop!

Every day we have prayer assignments; something you are to accomplish as you pray in the Holy Spirit. You do the praying and the Holy Spirit does the work.

We must make praying in the Holy Spirit a priority!

How many souls do you want to see transformed out of darkness into God's kingdom? How much victory do you want in your life? How much do you want to grow spiritually? It all depends on how willing you are to pray in the Holy Spirit. It all depends how much time you will commit to praying in the Spirit as well as your time in God's Word!

People are waiting for you to pray in the Holy Spirit and birth them into the kingdom! Jesus is expecting you to pray in the Holy Spirit so the lost ones, the broken ones can be saved healed and delivered!

Acts 6:4 we will give ourselves continually to prayer and to the ministry of the Word…

This must be our focus! This must be our vision! This must be our calling, our purpose to pray in the Holy Spirit, and to give ourselves to a life of prayer and the ministry of God's Word!

This is not for the passive or the lukewarm; this is for those who passionately and aggressively seek and love the Lord Jesus Christ!

Our success is directly connected to our prayer life. The greater the prayer life, the greater the success.

You may not know what your prayer assignment is, but the Holy Spirit does and as you pray in the Holy Spirit he will fulfill your assignment and give purpose to your life in Jesus name!

www.ingramcontent.com/pod-product-compliance
Lightning Source LLC
Chambersburg PA
CBHW061247040426
42444CB00010B/2276